The Developing

Artist

AUDIO
INCLUDED

Piano Literature Book 2
Original Keyboard Classics

REVISED EDITION

Early Intermediate

Original

Keyboard

Classics

T0057128

Compiled and edited by
Nancy and Randall Faber

Production: Frank and Gail Hackinson
Production Coordinator: Philip Groeber
Cover: Terpstra Design, San Francisco
Engraving: Tempo Music Press, Inc.

FABER
PIANO ADVENTURES®
3042 Creek Drive
Ann Arbor, Michigan 48108

THE PERIODS OF MUSIC HISTORY

BAROQUE

Dates: 1600–1750, a time of glittering royal courts in Europe, wigs on men, and the colonization of America.

Style: The word "Baroque" describes a very decorative style of art and architecture. Music of the Baroque period is often "decorated" with trills, turns, and other added notes.

Composers: Johann Sebastian Bach is the most famous of the Baroque composers. This book includes a piece from the *Notebook for Anna Magdalena Bach*, a set of pieces written by J.S. Bach and his friends and family. Another famous Baroque composer is Jean-Philipe Rameau. He was a French composer and harpsichordist who wrote an important text on music theory.

Performance: The harpsichord, clavichord, and organ were the keyboard instruments used during the Baroque period. (The piano was not invented until the early 1700s.)

CLASSICAL

Dates: Approximately 1750–1830, the time of the French and American Revolutions, Thomas Jefferson, and the rise and fall of Napoleon. Men still wore wigs and lace, bowed politely, and danced the minuet.

Style: The Classical period sought a return to simplicity and to what is "natural." The music is generally elegant and melodic.

Composers: Mozart, Haydn, and Beethoven were the major composers of the Classical period. This book includes a piece by Johann Christian Bach, one of J.S. Bach's sons. His music is very different from that of his father because he wrote in the new Classical style. J.C. Bach was an important teacher of the young Mozart.

Performance: The early piano was called the fortepiano. It became popular because it allowed the performer to play loud (forte) or soft (piano) tones by varying the touch. The fortepiano was a delicate instrument with a light, clear tone.

ROMANTIC

Dates: Approximately 1830–1910, a time of industrial growth in Europe and America, the Civil War in the United States, and Queen Victoria's reign over the British Empire.

Style: Romantic composers tried to express deep personal feelings in their music. As a result, harmonies, rhythm, and musical form became more complex.

Composers: Two important Romantic composers featured in this collection are Robert Schumann (Germany) and Peter Ilyich Tchaikovsky (Russia). Tchaikovsky composed the music for the famous ballet *The Nutcracker*.

Performance: Many consider the 19th century (1800s) to be the high point for solo piano music. The instrument, now called the pianoforte, was very similar to the piano of today. The performer could create "colors" at the piano through shadings of touch and pedal. A tasteful "give and take" in the rhythmic pulse, called *rubato*, is characteristic of the Romantic style.

CONTEMPORARY

Dates: 1900 to the present, the time of World Wars I and II, the development of the automobile and phonograph, putting man on the moon, and the invention of the computer.

Style: Modern music is wide and varied. Characteristics include dissonant harmonies, exciting rhythms, and a wide range of dynamics.

Composers: Russian and American composers are featured here. The Russian composer Rebikov was one of the earliest composers to experiment with 20th century musical ideas.

Performance: Experimentation has been a powerful force in 20th century music composition. For instance, today's pianist is sometimes asked to pluck the strings inside the piano, or to play clusters of notes with the palm of the hand. It is an exciting time for musicians as today's composers draw from the wealth of the past and set new trends for the future.

TABLE OF CONTENTS

King William's March

Jeremiah Clarke
(1674–1707)

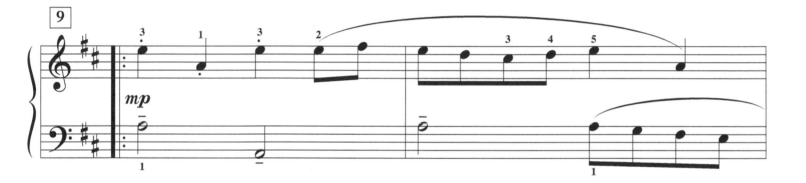

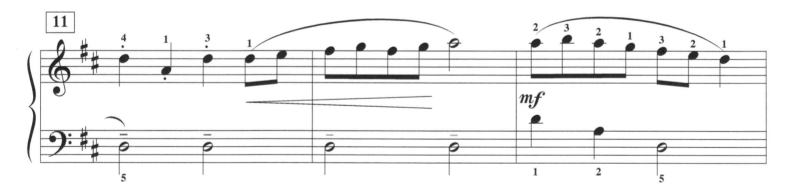

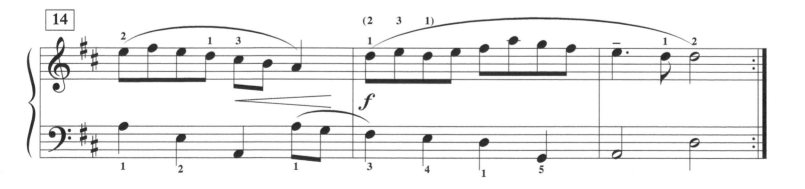

Minuet in G Major
(from the *Notebook for Anna Magdalena Bach*)

Christian Pezold
(1677–1733)

Gracefully

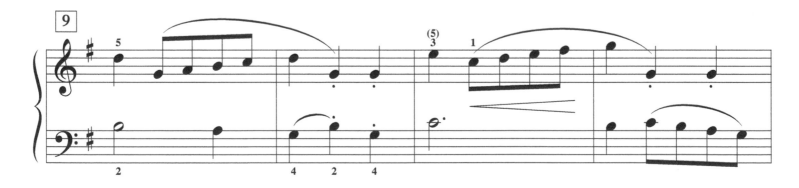

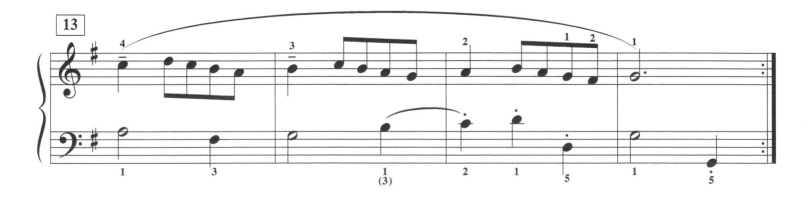

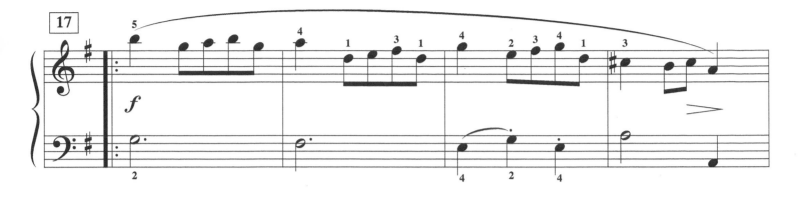

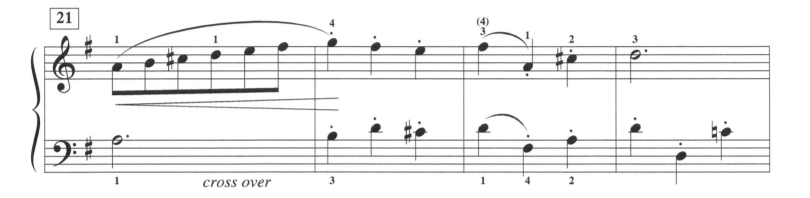

cross over

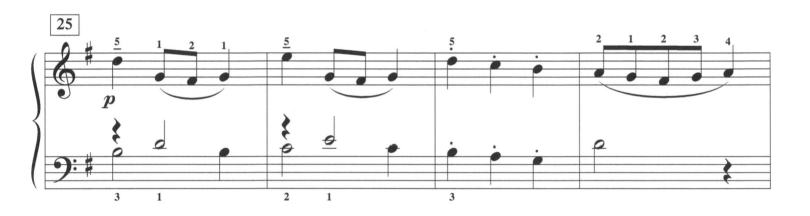

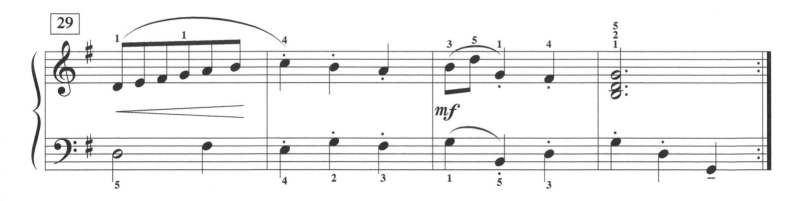

Menuet en Rondeau

Jean-Philippe Rameau
(1683–1764)

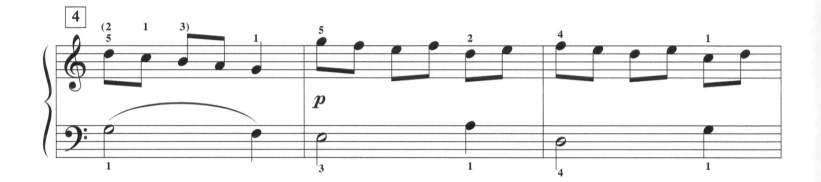

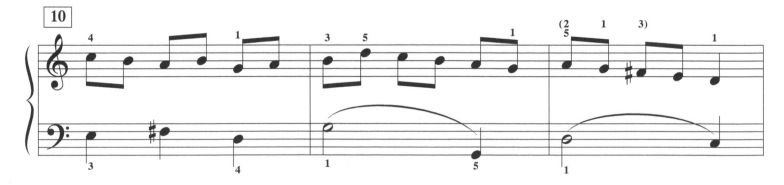

*It was common practice in music of the French Baroque to play the step-wise eighth notes with a slight lilt (in long-short pairs). This practice is known as *notes inégales* (unequal notes).

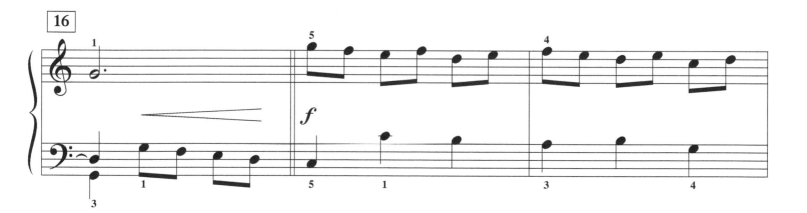

Air in D Minor

Daniel Speer
(1636–1707)

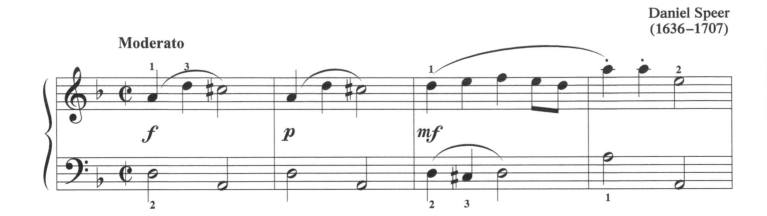

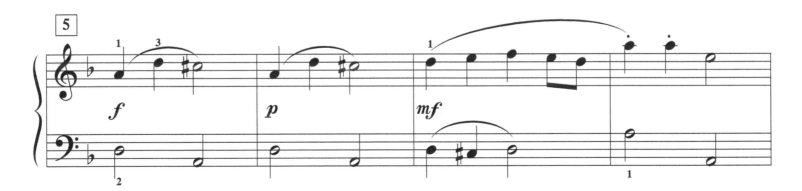

Bourrée

Christoph Graupner
(1683–1760)

CLASSICAL
1750 - circa 1830

Prelude in A Minor

Johann Christian Bach
(1735–1782)

Andante ♩ = 120

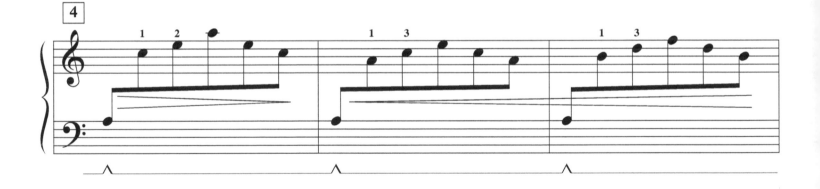

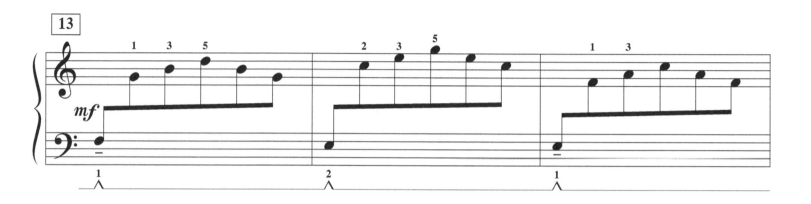

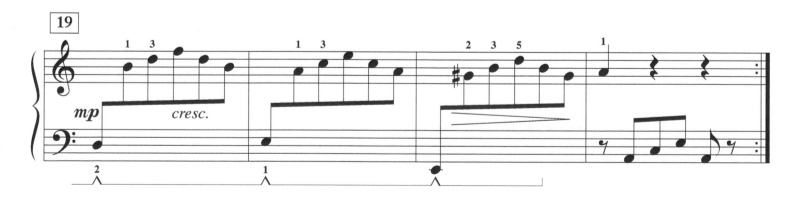

Dance in F Major

Wolfgang Amadeus Mozart
(1756–1791)

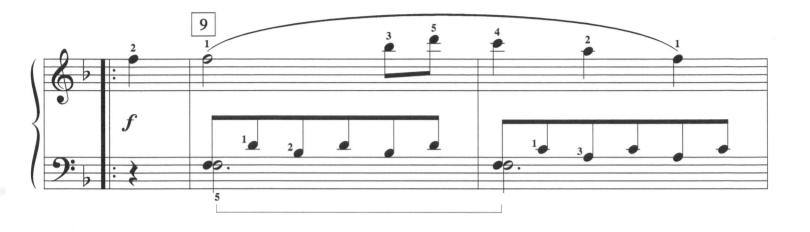

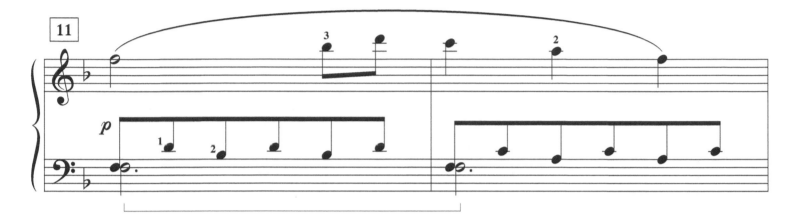

2nd time rit.

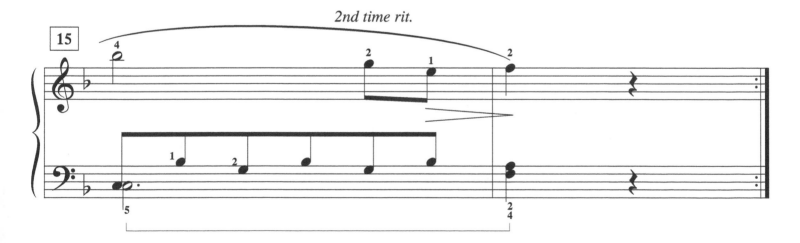

Minuet in C Major
(K. 6)

Wolfgang Amadeus Mozart
(1756–1791)

Moderato

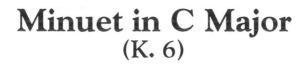

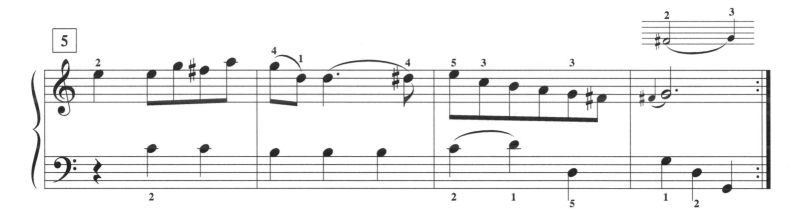

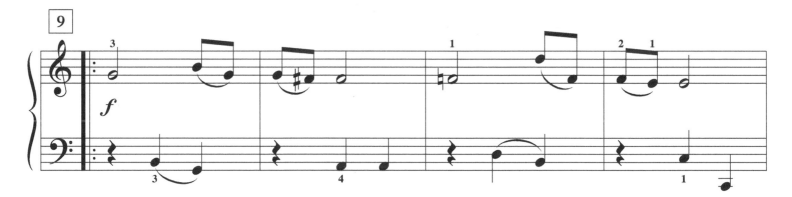

Russian Folk Dance

Ludwig van Beethoven
(1770–1827)

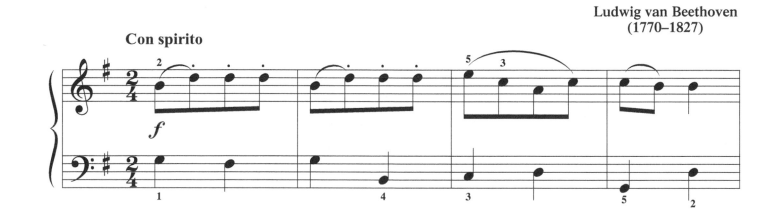

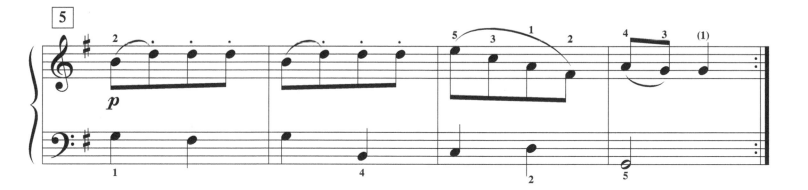

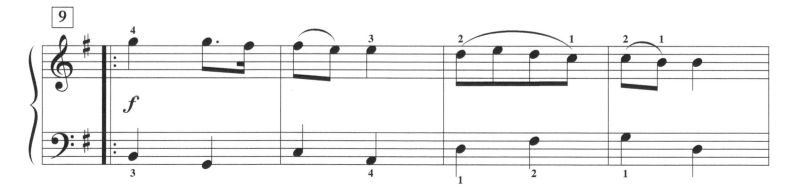

Ecossaise

Ludwig van Beethoven
(1770–1827)

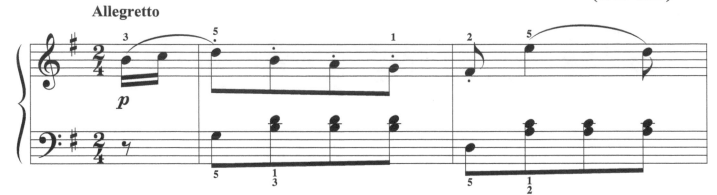

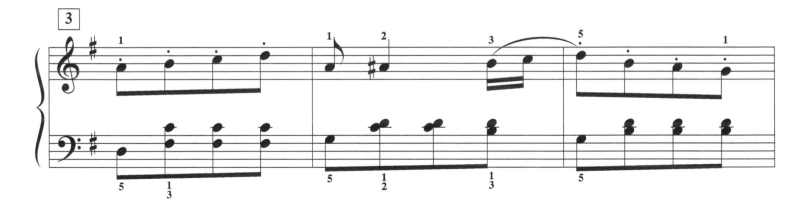

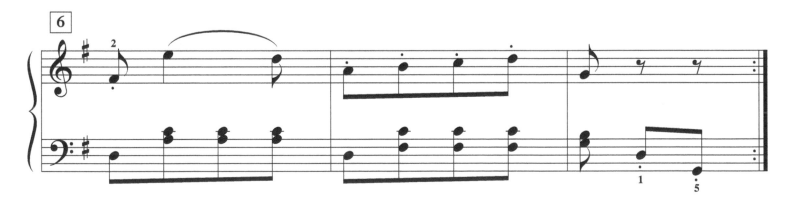

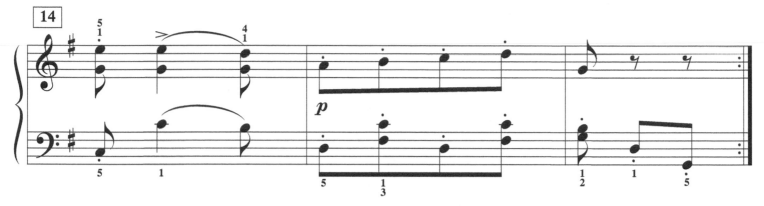

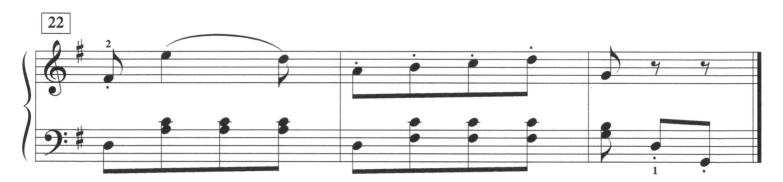

Sonatina in G Major

Ludwig van Beethoven
(1770–1827)

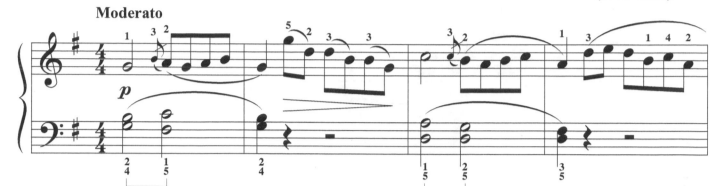

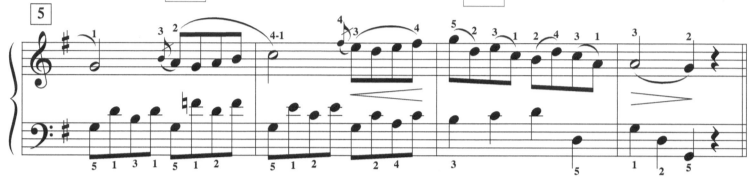

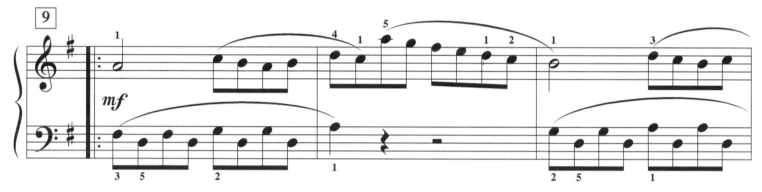

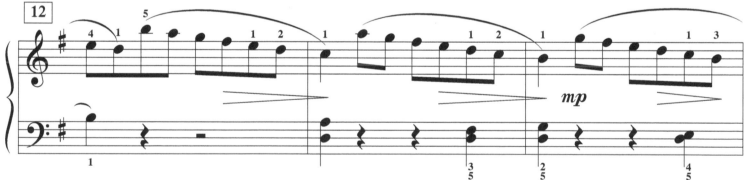

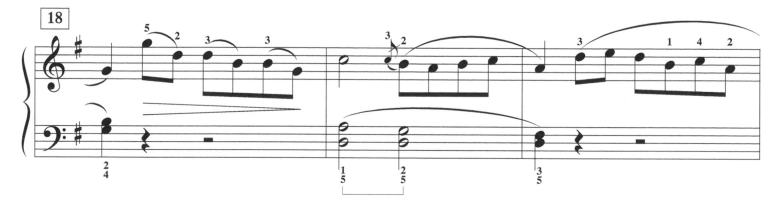

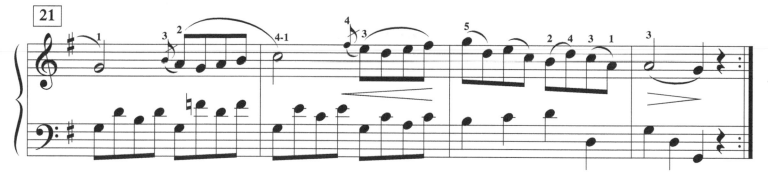

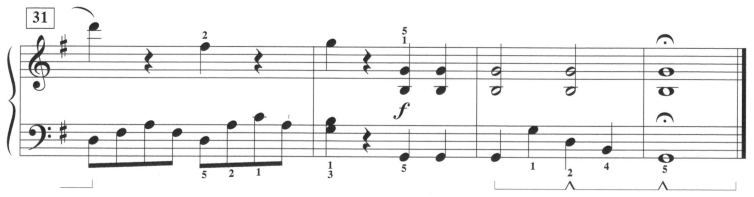

22

Romanze

Moderato

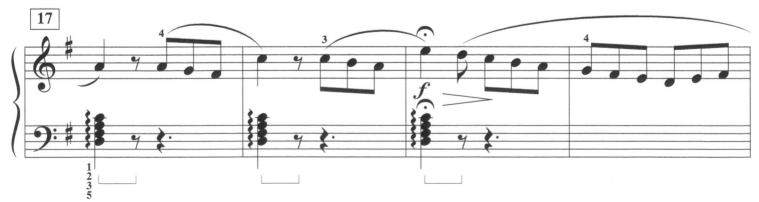

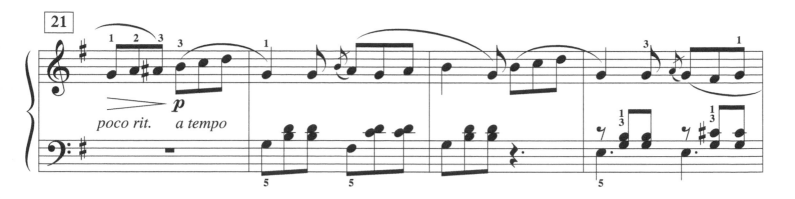

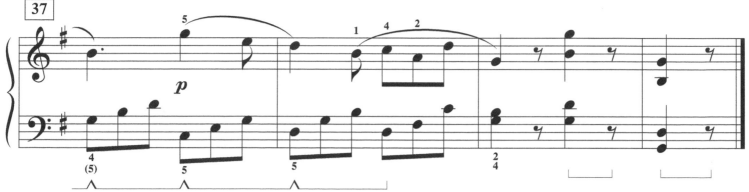

Teacher Part

Polka
(Opus 280, No. 2)
Secondo

Johann Hummel
(1778–1837)

Student Part

Polka
(Opus 280, No. 2)
Primo

Johann Hummel
(1778–1837)

Romantic
circa 1830–1910

Mazurka

Maria Szymanowska
(1790–1831)

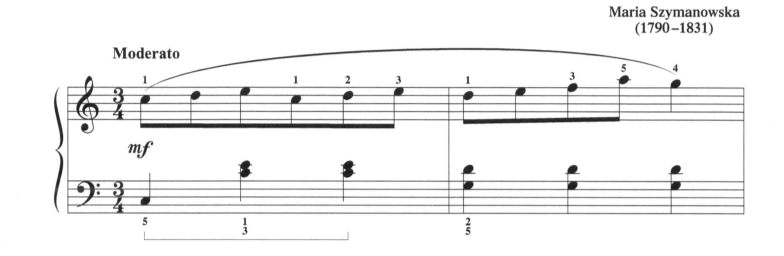

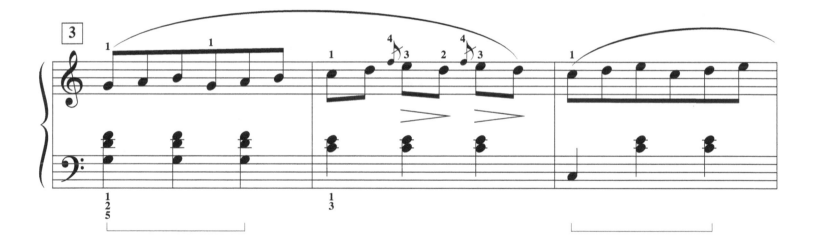

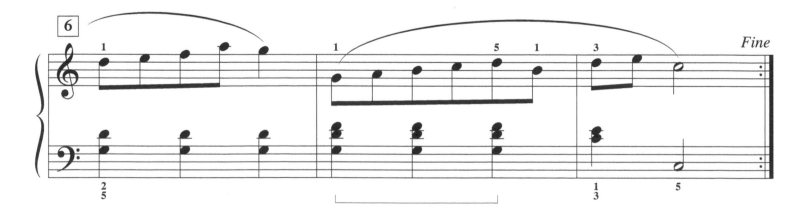

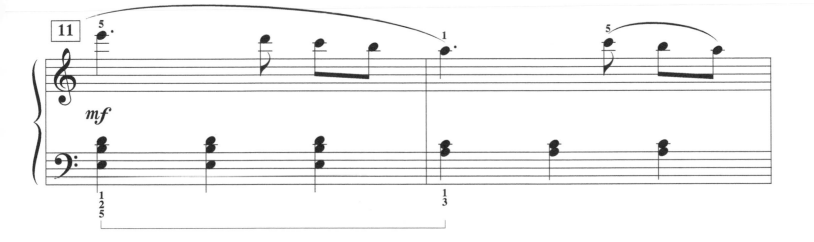

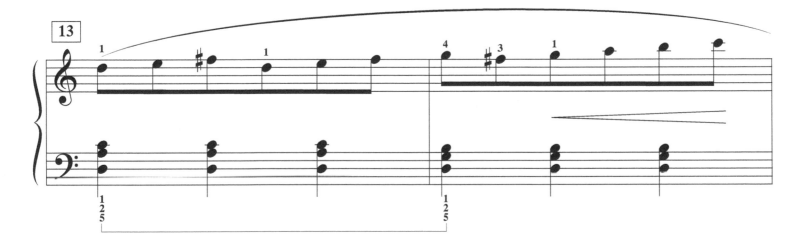

D.C. al Fine

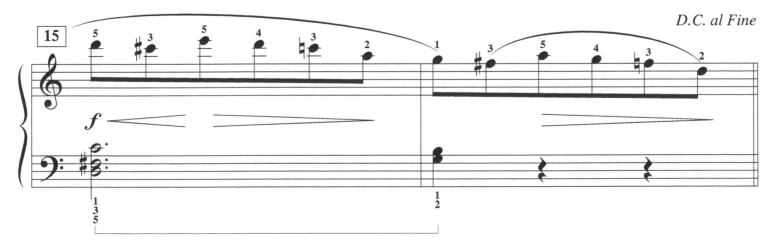

The Return
(Opus 117, No. 24)

Cornelius Gurlitt
(1820–1901)

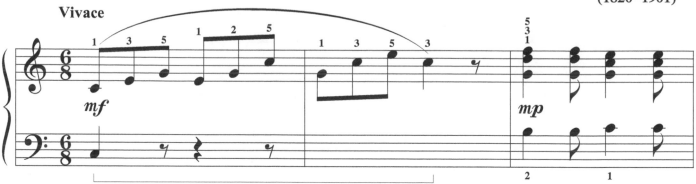

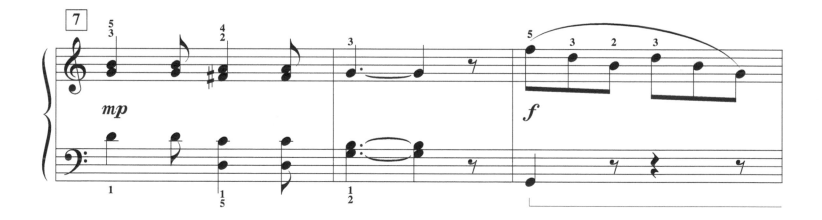

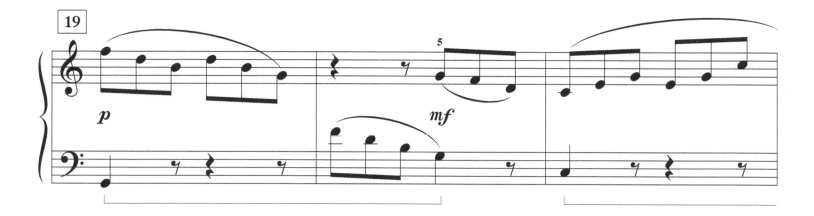

In the Garden
(Opus 140, No. 4)

Cornelius Gurlitt
(1820–1901)

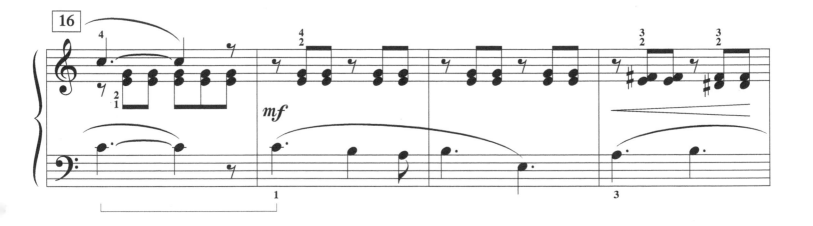

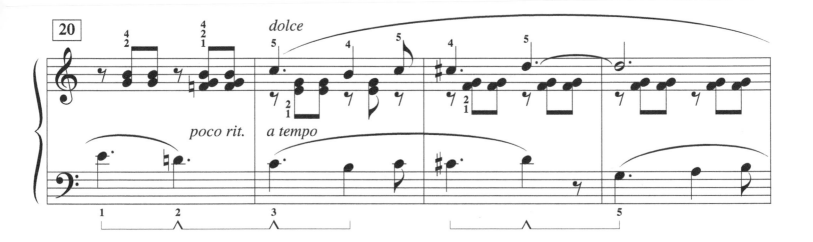

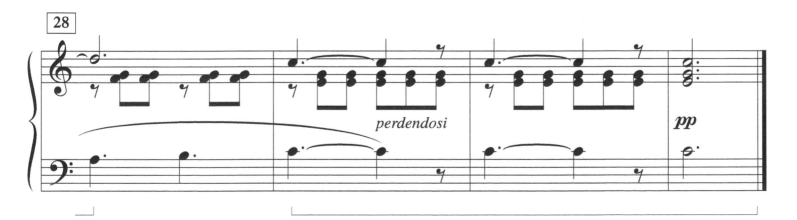

Soldier's March
(from *Album for the Young*, Opus 68, No. 2)

Robert Schumann
(1810–1856)

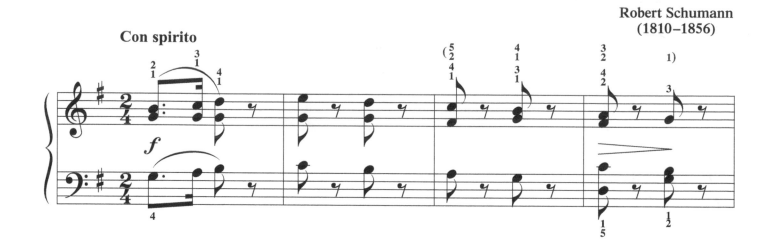

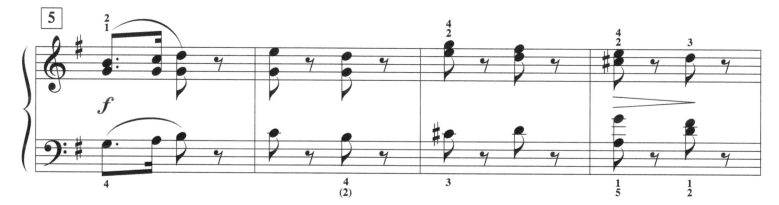

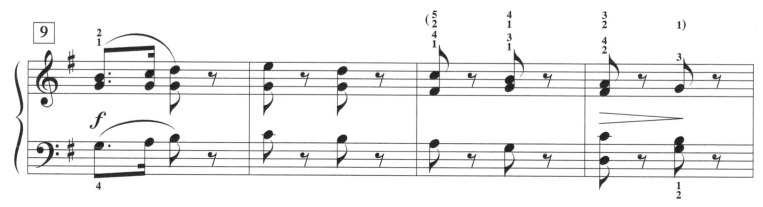

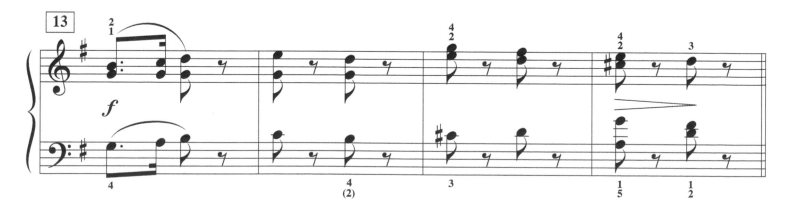

The Happy Farmer
(from *Album for the Young*, Opus 68, No. 10)

Robert Schumann
(1810–1856)

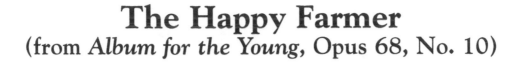

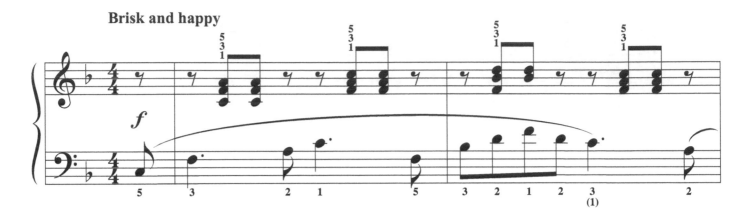

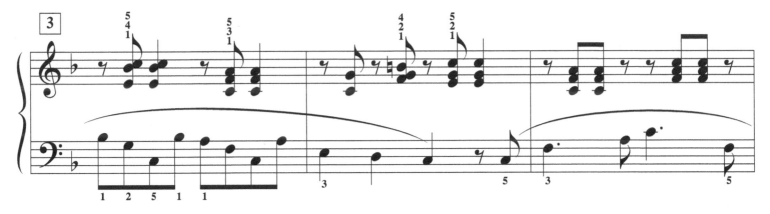

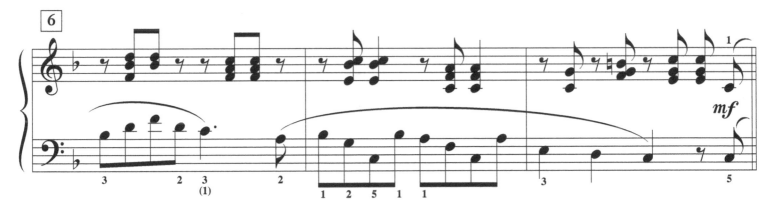

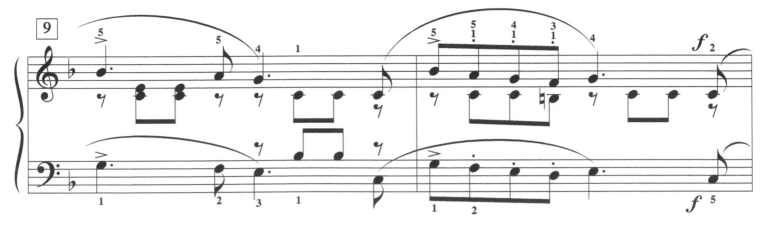

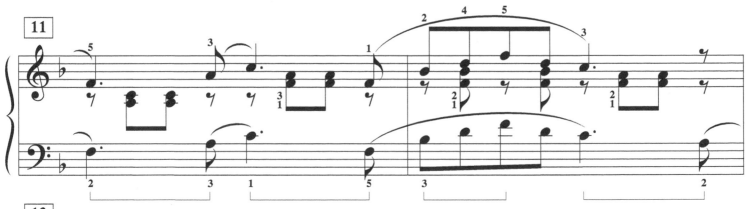

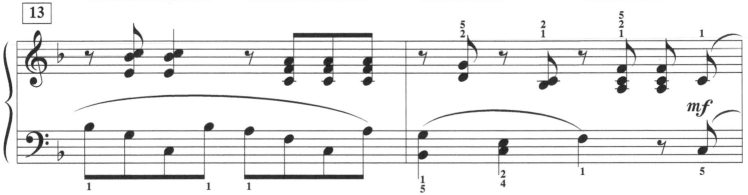

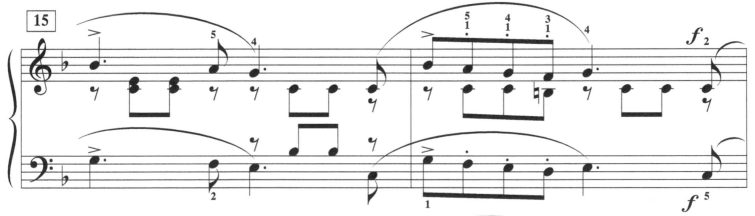

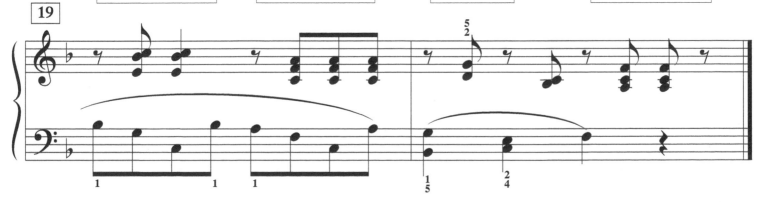

Old French Song
(from *Album for the Young*, Opus 39, No. 16)

Peter Ilyich Tchaikovsky
(1840–1893)

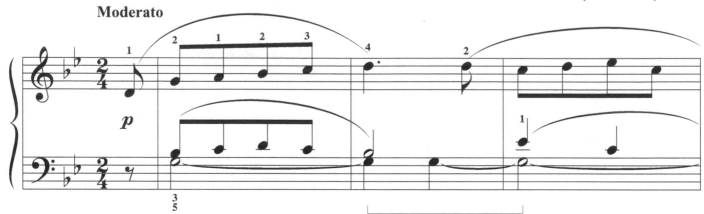

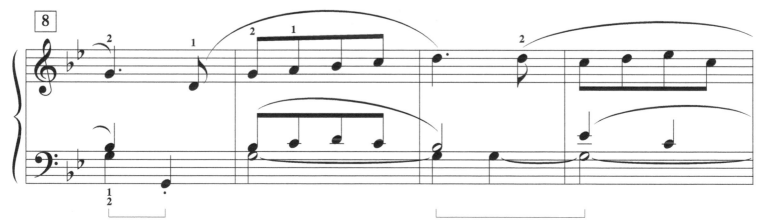

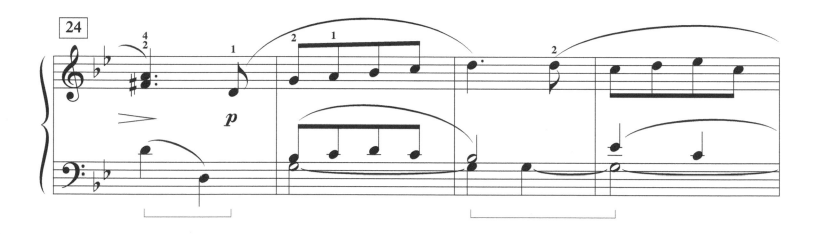

Contemporary
circa 1900–present

Long Gone Blues
Ghost Town Memories
from *Sagebrush Country*, No. 8

George Frederick McKay
(1899–1970)

Freely in blues tempo (♩ = 80)

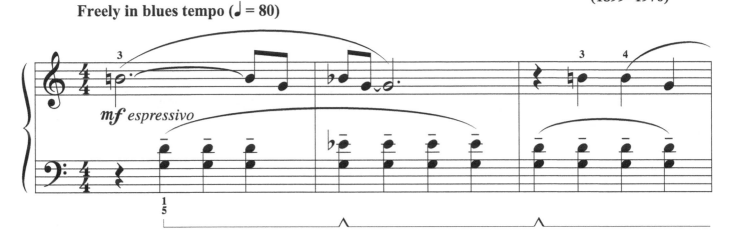

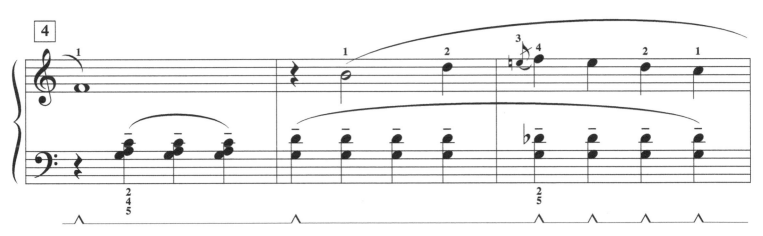

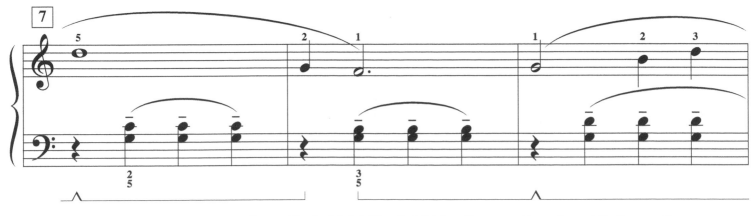

FF1034

The Bear

Vladimir Rebikov
(1866–1920)

Waltz Macabre
(Bitonal Waltz)

Nancy Faber
(1955–)

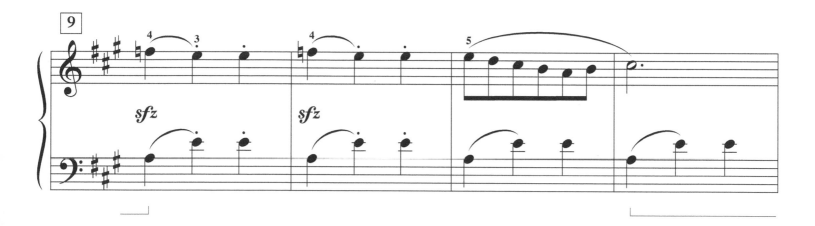

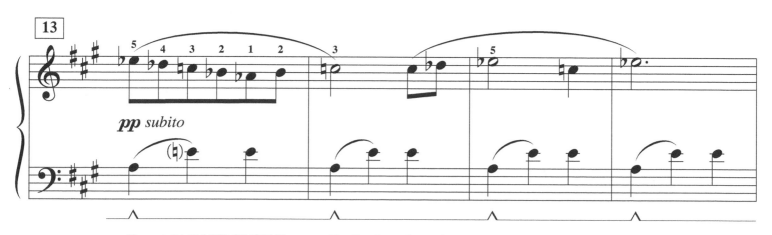

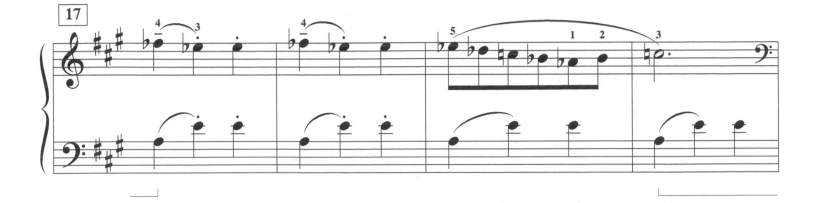

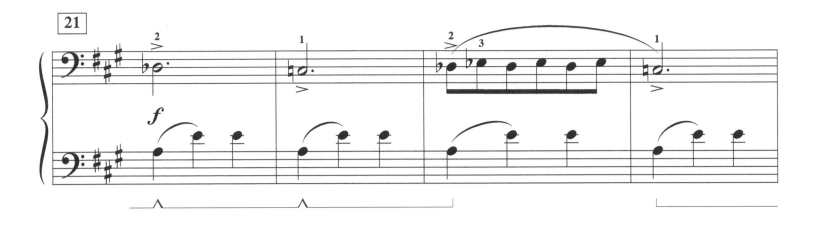

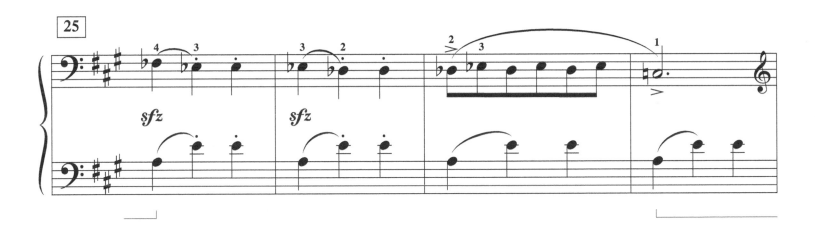

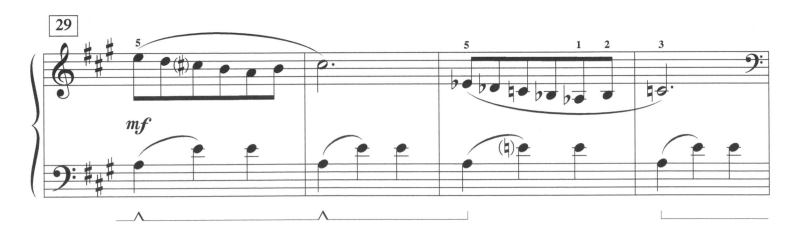

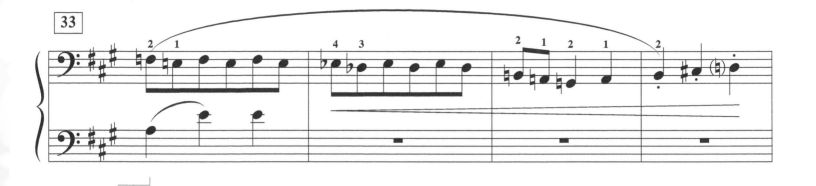

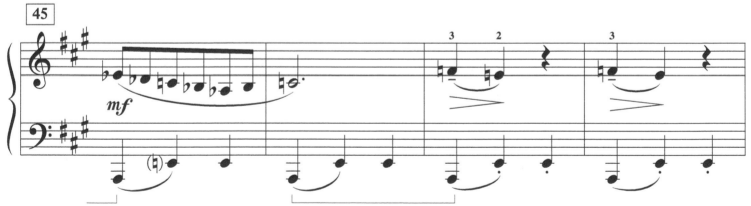

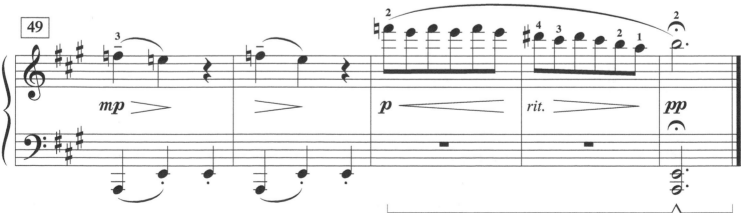

Yiki

A Mesopotamian Elephant
(from Safari)

John Robert Poe
(1926-2004)

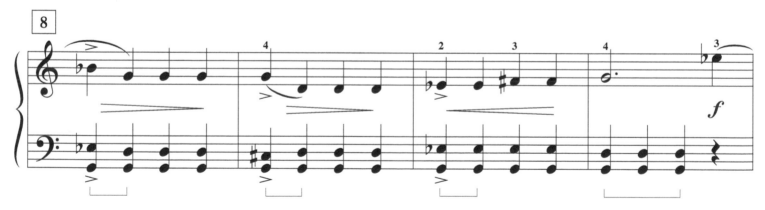

*Play a loud, white-key cluster on the four lowest keys; then depress the sostenuto pedal (middle pedal) to sustain. (If your piano does not have a sostenuto pedal, play mm. 1–4, treble clef, with the right hand.)

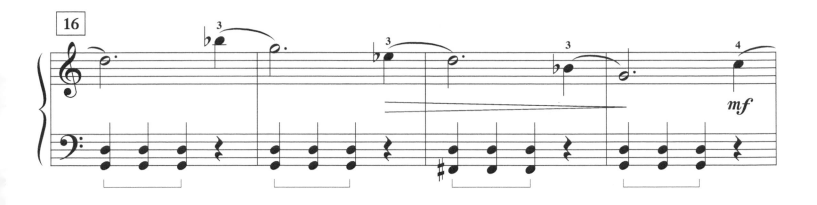

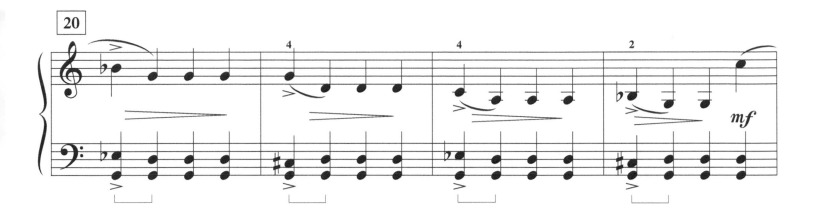

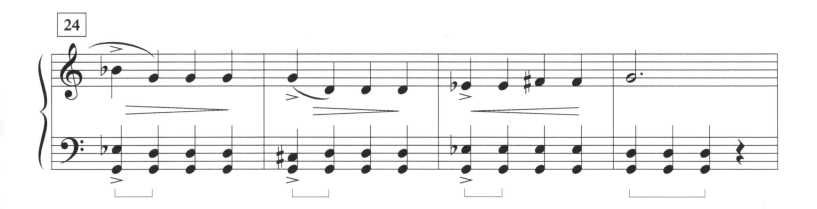

DICTIONARY OF MUSICAL TERMS

DYNAMIC MARKS

pp	*p*	*mp*	*mf*	*f*	*ff*
pianissimo	*piano*	*mezzo piano*	*mezzo forte*	*forte*	*fortissimo*
very soft	soft	moderately soft	moderately loud	loud	very loud

crescendo (cresc.)
Play gradually louder.

diminuendo (dim.) or decrescendo (decresc.)
Play gradually softer.

TEMPO MARKS

Adagio	*Andante*	*Moderato*	*Allegretto*	*Allegro*	*Vivace*
slowly	"walking speed" (slower than *Moderato*)	moderate tempo	rather fast	fast and lively	very fast

SIGN	TERM	DEFINITION
	a tempo	Return to the beginning tempo (speed).
$\downarrow$	**accent**	Play this note louder.
	andantino	A little faster than *andante*.
	air	A melodic or song-like instrumental piece.
	bitonal	In two different keys at the same time.
	bourrée	A French dance from the 17th century. A bourrée is in $\frac{2}{4}$ or $\frac{4}{4}$ time with an upbeat (pick-up note).
C	**common time**	$\frac{4}{4}$ time. The ♩ gets one beat. Four beats per measure.
¢	**cut time (alla breve)**	$\frac{2}{2}$ time. The ♩ gets one beat. Two half-note beats per measure.
	con spirito	With spirit.
	D.C. al Fine	*Da Capo al Fine*. Return to the beginning and play until *Fine*.
	dolce	Sweetly.
	ecossaise	A lively country dance in $\frac{2}{4}$ time.
	espressivo	Expressively.
⌒	*fermata*	Hold this note longer than usual.
	Fine	End here.
	Köchel	L. van Köchel made a chronological listing of all of Mozart's works. Köchel numbers (K.) are used instead of opus numbers for Mozart's compositions.

	legato	Smoothly connected.
	marcato il canto	Stress the melody.
	mazurka	A Polish folk dance in $\frac{3}{4}$ time.
	menuet	French for "minuet."
	minuet	A stately dance in $\frac{3}{4}$ time.
	musette	A piece that imitates a bagpipe.
	Notebook for Anna Magdalena Bach	A collection of pieces by J.S. Bach, his sons, and friends, presented to his wife Anna Magdalena as a gift.
Op.	**opus**	A creative work. A composer's pieces are often numbered in the order in which they were written. Each work is given an *opus* number. Several pieces may be included in a single opus. For example, Op. 3, No. 1; Op. 3, No. 2, etc.
8va — ¬	*ottava*	Play one octave higher than written. When 8va – ⌐ is below the staff, play one octave lower than written.
	perdendosi	Dying away.
	poco	A little. For example, *poco rit.* means a little *ritard*.
	poco a poco	Little by little.
	primo	The treble part in a four-hand piano duet.
rit.	*ritardando*	Gradually slow down.
	romanze	A short piece with a lyrical (expressive) character.
	rondeau	French predecessor of the rondo.
	rondo	A musical form featuring a recurring A section.
	secondo	The bass part (second part) in a four-hand piano duet.
	sempre	Always. For example, *sempre staccato* means *staccato* throughout.
	simile	Similarly. For example, *Ped. simile* means to continue pedaling in the same manner.
	slur	Connect the notes over or under a slur.
	sonatina	A little *sonata*. (A *sonata* is a type of instrumental piece.)
	staccato	Play notes marked *staccato* detached, disconnected.
	tempo di Marcia	March tempo.
	tenuto mark (stress mark)	Hold this note its full value. Stress the note by pressing gently into the key.

ALPHABETICAL INDEX OF TITLES

Access audio online at
pianoadventures.com/lit2
password: **9a3k8x**

For technical support, visit
pianoadventures.com/contact